Diary Poems

and

Story Teller's Rhymes

Diary Poems

and

Story Teller's Rhymes

Sonjoy Dutta-Roy

AuthorHouse™
1663 Liberty Drive
Bloomington, IN 47403
www.authorhouse.com
Phone: 1-800-839-8640

Published by AuthorHouse   07/30/2012

ISBN: 978-1-4772-1534-0 (sc)
ISBN: 978-1-4772-1535-7 (e)

Poet, Theatre person, Professor, University of Allahabad, India, Author of The Absent Words and Into Grander Space

Praise for The Absent Words (Gautam Siddharth in The Pioneer, New Delhi, January 4 1999):

Dutta-Roy travels through quality time, preserves energy and carries very little excess baggage . . . frugal in one, immodest in another, lonely in one, boisterous in another, his poems acutely reflect the times he has lived through.

Praise for Into Grander Space (Makarand Paranjape in Kavya Bharati, Madurai, no.18, 2006):

The epic and the lyric modes intertwine to create a vast sweep in both time and space. Temporally going back into prehistoric mythic times, the poem comes right into the present. Considering that very few long poems are written anywhere these days, Dutta-Roy must be congratulated on this effort. This is a noble moving, even a charming poem in parts.

Contents

Diary Poems and Story Teller's Rhymes, continues two traditions of poetry into contemporary times: a.) the oral tradition where fables, parables and myths are narrated in rhymed verse, both for instruction and entertainment; b.) the introspective and reflective written tradition where deep personal concerns emerge in heightened rhythm and rhyme, through images, metaphors and symbols.

This book blends these two traditions, maintaining a distinction all the time. Some of the fables are originally created out of contemporary issues. "Poach Tantra" takes up the problem of poaching through an animal fable in the Panchtantra tradition. Others like "The Snake Story", "The Comet Avatar", and the "Katha Serial Saga" (a contemporary retake on the frame story of *Kathasaritasagar*) are remakes of ancient myths to suit the contemporary times. The *Diary Poems* are actually diary poems preserved through a period of intense personal crisis and transition. Together with the *Story Teller's Rhymes* they try to juxtapose the complex and intricate relationship between the objective and the subjective worlds in which we simultaneously exist. For example "Curtain Calls" is a meditation after the death of the poet's parents in quick succession in 2010. "Poach Tantra", that follows, is a grandfather's tale to a granddaughter from an earlier date. At the same time one sincerely hopes that they are able to continue into these troubled contemporary times, and in an age dominated by prose and reason, the wonder and beauty and possibilities of poetry as narrative and poetry as introspection.

This is a book of poems that contains fables, myths and parables. Stories have always fascinated audiences and readers. India has a rich heritage of stories that have been tapped into. These stories can appeal both to children and adults anywhere in the world where English is read and understood. The diary poems have a subtler appeal for the more perceptive poetry readers.

Curtain Calls

(Rituals: Across Time and Space)
(August 2010: To my parents who left in
quick succession)

A storm howled through the house for months
An old house shaken to its foundation
And a lost breeze weeps through the windowpanes
Chasing a whirlwind of ghosts through the by lanes
That shoot across the city's distant horizon
Or flutters on the glass like a trapped moth
As the raindrops mist the eyes of the sun.

An eerie silence descends, and a vast emptiness.
It is night and there is not a wink of sleep in my eyes.
In this dark night of sadness, you come
You come to me, Oh my stark God of loneliness
As the lightning streaks the sky asunder
Striking the darkness unconscious with its thunder
That knocks on my rattling doors.

I will open them wide and let you in
Oh stranger, my ever welcome stranger
In this dark night of sorrow
Come Oh come to my house my friend
What message do you bring at the hours end
Come, my dear composite ghost, from land's end

And we will share our half drunk bottle of rum
And from you Poet God's sacred text
Sing a full song, or half a melody hum.

The bottle lies empty
The songs reverberate into the echoing silence
That descends as the storm recedes into the blurred edges
    of night and day.
The composite ghost has departed, how could they stay
As the sun dawns across my lunar half drunk pretence.
The house lies empty.
The beam from the skylight
Brings the imprint on the sofa in the spotlight
Light, curtain calls and departure!

The script gets scattered from a heap
Fluttering in the whirr of a rotating breeze
Directorial instructions encrypted deep
The last scene etched in an eternal freeze.
Spotlights, music and the final overture!
Before the exit through the wings

Oh still that farewell gesture!

Come My Friend in this Hour of Change . . .

When the burning lava starts cooling
Flow in me like the fertile sap of compassion.
When the crackling fire starts dying
Glow in me like the passionate ash of reflection.
When the consuming tide starts receding
Slow soak into me the embracing ocean's retention.
When the dancing cyclone starts returning
Blow into me its epicentral eye's dissolution.
When the glacial avalanche starts melting
Grow in me like the silting flood's deposition.

Come my friend in this inevitable hour of change
As youth fades into insignificance, passion dissolves,
And as the song goes:
"Your snaking plaits do not dance and sway
To the charming breeze's hypnotic sway
No lightning streaks across your eyes
When the thunder rumbles in the skies"
And teach me the song of the weather beaten face
Teach me the dance of the slow motioned grace
Teach me to paint with the sun's fading trace
Teach me the quiet of the silent space
Teach me to master your disappearing act,
And tease me into your final embrace.

The Poach Tantra
Or
The Poaching Saga

In the open spaces where the dholes* run free
Where the gaurs* and cheetals* graze happily
The tiger stretches under the huge sal tree
The sloth bear feeds on the ants merrily.

Deep inside the slushy swampland
You can hear the frog and the cicada band
The gharial* basks on the riverbank sand
And the elephants blow their trumpets grand

Up on the mountain, in the forest glade
The stealthy leopard finds its shade
On the jutting cliffs, the vultures parade
The cataract descends in a sweeping cascade.

The paradise fly catcher gleams in the light
The peacock dances, its feathers alight
The python and the cobra slide out of sight
The herons scream, in the twilight.

After the last wood bark is drilled
After the last tiger is killed
After the cicada band is stilled
After the last deer is grilled
After the last feather is plucked
After the last leather wallet is tucked.

A child might ask her grandfather:
"Sing me the lullaby
Where the dholes run free
And the bear eats merrily"

"Take me to the land
Of the frog and cicada band
Of the basking gharials on the sand"

"Show me the sight
Of a flycatcher in flight
Of dancing peacock feathers alight."

And so, before such a tragedy befalls
Grandpa from memory a story recalls:

"Dear child that land could be no more
Just the lullaby remain
The tragic after of a terrible before
And its sad melancholy strain"

Sonjoy Dutta-Roy

"Like in the tale in Panchatantra
Or in Aesop's famous fable
These creatures tried the magic mantra
Of a dialogue around a wooded table"

"They were facing a serious problem
Some things were terribly wrong
How were they to solve them?
It was not going to be a song"

"Tigers disappearing, elephants dead, tusks dismembered
Rhinos slayed, peacocks fatally defeathered
Who could be so powerful, huge, ruthlessly unfettered
Who, not out of hunger, but out of greed, slaughtered?"

"After a four hours deliberation
To a consensus did they arrive
It could be no less than a revolution
That could ensure that they survive"

"But first and foremost, and most important
This hidden and cunning monster,
This slimy ghost, horrible giant
Should be caught and controlled, stirrup and holster"

"And so an army of hooded owls
Who flew the woods at night
And a pack of golden dholes
Who ran the meadows in the light

Were set out on secret prowls
To spot and report, when they caught sight
Of the horrible, elusive, bloodthirsty ghouls"

"The strategy, as it was planned
Was first to get the lay of the land
Spot the culprits in red hand
And unobserved observe
The secret ways of this marauding band"

"And so it happened that on a fateful day
A jackal trotting his wayward way
Chanced upon this familiar creature
Call him what you may
Two legged, smelling strange, with peculiar fur
How did he in this forest stray?"

"Unnoticed, our jackal watched
This man in his deep purpose engrossed
Digging what seemed like a massive pit
Which later he covered bit by bit
With sticks, straw, grass, earth, grit
In a perfectly disguised natural fit"

"Our hero of the day, puzzled to the core
Went to report to the wise wild boar
Who, with grim visage, a snort and a roar
Announced:
'This was serious matter

Which one needed to further explore
So all the spies should later scatter
To the fringes and the forest border
Keep eyes glued to the village cluster
And return with stories, more and more
About this mysterious two legged creature
Who smelt so strange, such funny furs wore"'

"And it was no laughing matter
As by and by, they were to find later
This weak and defenseless apelike fellow
Had more inside his skull's hollow
Than all of them put together"

"And sure enough in a week's time
A tiger, a leopard, a bear in his prime
Just disappeared into thin air
Leaving hollows in the deep pit's grime
Connecting our cunning ape with the crime"

"A second meeting was urgently called
All jungle activity effectively stalled
And all the creatures great and small,
Bright and beautiful,
Wise and wonderful
Pitched in all knowledge, information all
About this all powerful two legged know all"

"Mysterious facts came to light
About this creature's greed and his might
He was the owner of a third hand
That poured fire, pain, sleep and death
Do you understand?
And after that, to add to the fright
The hyenas revealed a gruesome sight
Of a huge pachyderm killed at night
His tusks scavenged
Leaving raw flesh and many a blood strand"

"Fur, tooth, claw and eyes
Of any shape or any size
For this monster became a coveted prize
They fetched for him an unimaginable price"

"Price? question marks in every eye
'Yes, dear friends, I will tell you the what and the why'
Said the sly fox, who beyond the fringe did often stray
And knew more of this creature's way
By leading some of the dogs astray"

"With goats, elephants, buffalos and cows
The dogs answered the whys and the hows
Abandoning all their domestic vows"

"The grazing goats, buffalos and cows
Munching away in the meadows high
Whispered secrets to the passing nilgai"

"The chained elephant by the river's side
Sending a coded trumpet tried
To his wild brethren on the other side"

"Village dogs raised their midnight howl
To dholes and wolves out on the prowl"

"And here was the crux of the matter
Heard from the tongue of our fox trotter":

"'There is this mysterious piece of paper
Of which this human is very fond
This from the codes can we decipher
As we sit around this moonlit pond'"

"It was like any other paper
Some smaller in size, some bigger
Not food, nor fruit, nor fire, nor water
Not honey, nor wood, nor stone, nor heather,
Just a piece of rectangular paper
And there was such an insane clamber,
Rush, race, cunning and murder
For more and more of it to gather
Brain and muscle were used together
To buy more and more and more power
Through rupees, euros and the great dollar
For that was what they called this paper
The company was told by our fox scholar":

"'The strange equation of zero and infinity
Works itself through this magical rupee
Do not underrate its capability'"

"'It can destroy a forest and buy it
It can control a river and dam it
It can drill the earth and tap it
It can pierce the sky and map it
It can mushroom into a fireball
Destroying every one and all

Just a piece of little paper-zero value
Could create an infinite hullabaloo'"

"'So where do we stand, puny creatures
With our furs, claws, teeth and other features'"

"A pall of gloom on our company spread
The bottom of their hearts filled with dread
There seemed to be no reasonable room
For anything other than impending doom"

"With heads bowed and tails tucked
Feathers drooping, all vitality sucked
To their respective homes they trudged
And for a full long endless night
From their liars, holes, dens, nobody budged"

Sonjoy Dutta-Roy

"Except the perky lapwing
Who carried the night on its wing
Testing her dubious ability to sing
Even though the world was ending"

"In her innumerable tangential trips
She had clearly observed these two legged creeps
They were not all the same, but of different breeds
With different luxuries and different needs"

"Some liked palaces, some liked the hills
Some liked limousines, some liked two wheels
Some liked cities, full of concrete
Some liked nature, sea and tree complete
Some liked blinkers, red lights and blue
Some liked just, to vanish into the blue
Some liked power, its trappings and all
Some liked the forest, its freedom call
Some liked animals, birds, bees et al
Dead and taxidermed, decorating their hall
Some liked them in the wild, having a ball"

"On such thoughts our lapwing lapped all night
Till she saw the sun's first new light
And as the morning came out bright
Of a distant hope she caught sight"

"She decided to whistle around the hermit's cave
In bird song to him this message she gave
There was no one else but he who could save
The flora and fauna of this forest enclave"

"The hermit woke up from his deep meditation
Plonked down to the ground from his levitation
And addressed our lapwing without hesitation":

"'Deep in the forest exists a tribe
Who, with this piece of paper, you cannot bribe
They have no earthly use for it
On the forest and its gifts subsist
I will tell them how their own species
Of the towns, villages and the cities
Are scalping the forests and the seas.

They are sure to bring justice and peace
And get in touch with others overseas
And you in turn go back to your base
And report to me when you hear of a case'"

"That day the lapwing her story told
To the full company gathered in the fold
Let me to you the moral unfold":

Larger forces that we can perceive
Are working through us, we hardly conceive
This man who is a destroyer
Can be savior and a preserver.
Creation could be left, to the forces diverse
That spin the earth, and the uni-verse
And make me spin this yarn in verse

"That is where our saga now stands
I place it dear child, in your tender hands
For your memory's safe custody
To sing to the future in full melody"

*The Dhole is the wild dog of the Indian forest, the Gaur
is the huge Indian Bison, the Cheetal is the spotted deer
and the Gharial is the long snouted Indian crocodile.

The Snake Story

The snake, dear friends, is a curious creature. For no fault of its own it has assumed the satanic form of a tempter and seducer, leading to the fall from a state of spiritual grace into a state of bodily lowliness. But there is an ancient twist in the tale that gives the snake its due and proper justice. Interestingly it is a women's version embedded in the folk imagination working on a creation myth. Barring the phallic symbolism and the snake's preference for the dark and moist pits and holes in the netherworld, I cannot find any plausible rhyme or reason for this curious tendency to equate the snake with sexuality and bodily damnation and punishment. But here, as we sit under the ramparts of this Medieval fort built by Akbar, on the banks of the confluence of two powerful rivers, I can see a snake (a huge Cobra) peep out from the tangled boughs of the ancient Akshay Vat as it curls around the solid stones of this grand structure built to defend a civilized city from the onslaughts of savage marauding enemies. And interestingly, it was a snake whose body was used for the churning of the milk ocean as nectar and poison got separated. And does not this earth, even as it rotates, rest precariously on the head of the vast Shesh Naga. So, before my tale snakes around some more mythical oddities, let me bind you within the rhymed coils of a folk version of an ancient creation myth. It will tell you how the snake came to dwell simultaneously in the deadly depths of the netherworld and the heavenly heights of Shiva's entangled curls and Parvati's peaks. So let me chant the creation myth:

Having deceived Adishakti out of her lust
And reducing her to ashes and dust
Mahadeo revived Brahma and Vishnu
From their ashes back into their shapes they grew.
From the remains of Adishakti's powers he drew
Three feminine forms they could easily subdue,
For Adishakti's powerful sexuality
Had scared this primal male trinity.

Well, then, to cut a long story short,
They proceeded to create, each with his consort,
The various worlds, bird, beasts, insects, humans, demons,
    gods of all sorts
And finally when the entire job was done
They were summoned to an assembly, one by one,
And Mahadeo delivered the famous sermon:
"Children, you will not suffer hunger or thirst
Nor after each other will you obscenely lust
The fruits, flowers, trees, I give in full trust
Plundering and feasting will bring death and disease
The happy eternity will forever cease".

Chorus/Viveka:

Oh! When will eternity burst into time?
Is the release of pent up desires a crime?
What a curse it is to be caught in your prime
In a web of abstinence and fasting sublime

Let me take a little break from the creation story to ponder on Shiva's sermon. Of course he forbade eating fruits, plucking flowers and felling trees, or eating each other. But did he forbid sexual indulgence? Maybe the symbolic subtext behind the containing of hunger and the consuming instinct does hint at sexual control. Well, today when we look at what is happening all around, Mahadeo's words certainly hold deep meaning and there was ominous foreboding. But what I do not understand is why was the snake singled out of all creatures to drive this point home, and in several cultures? But let us continue with the story and the chant and maybe the answer lies right there:

Unfortunately the hen laid an egg, soft and round
The snake eyed it from the hole in the ground
Felt a desire in his blood, strong, sure and sound
To lick it and suck it, his tongue forked around
But Mahadeo's sermon lurked in the background.
Poor chap, he recoiled back to the soft coils
From which the head had risen, like a lunging foil.
Back he went to an uneasy serenity
The egg was a tempting serendipity
That refused to vanish from his mental faculty.
Of he slid in a zigzagged course
The Devas he engaged in a complex discourse:
"Could they not read through Mahadeo's deceit?
To live in abundance, excess and surfeit
To feel in the loins and the stomach albeit
An inflaming kind of desire concrete

And yet give it all up, everything forfeit
For some stagnant eternity, with boredom replete".

This did not cut ice with the Devas
Who wondered what all this fuss was
That came snaking into their vicinity
To disturb their peace and their tranquility.

Sure enough, they shooed him away
To the humans and demons he then made his way
And there he had his full say and sway
As they listened wrapped in curiosity
To the reptile's tantalizing verbosity.
Hypnotized by the hooded sway of words
They felt in their veins, and in their innards
Sensations strange and stirrings awkward sssssss . . . .

Chorus/Viveka:

Oh! The flesh, it has its own will
From its confines, the sap, it wants to swill
Over and flow, in its course across times
Multiplying and creating, as it twirls and twines
Consumes and spills, with pleasures sublime.

What lay curled at the base of the spine
In the stomach's pit, in the roots of the vine,
Dormant, supine,
Uncurled like a spring, it raised its head

What followed was an orgy, unprecedented
A feast and a carnival, unmitigated
Leaving its spoils all around
For Mahadeo to discover, sure and sound.

The surface of Heaven was grotesquely scarred
By dirt, seed and shit, blatantly marred
Mahadeo's wrath their act incurred
In the form of a curse, irreversibly disbursed
Off, they were hounded to a place called Earth
Enmeshed in the cycle of death and birth.

The demons and mortals lay forth their case
And blamed the snake, who lay at the base.
The snake was duly summoned from his sleep
Into Shiva's presence did he slither and creep.
Into the Netherworld was he cruelly cursed
But he was not to be so easily dispersed.

To justify his unruly act with the egg
He argued with Mahadeo till the last leg
And fair and square, he won his case
And managed to slide out of a state of disgrace.

The curse could not be reversed
So Mahadeo in compensation this clause reimbursed
The snake would have a double existence
The netherworld he would inhabit for subsistence
But Shiva's neck he would adorn as his true inheritance
And sway his head in this sublime presence.

What, you ask, was the snake's argument
That swayed Mahadeo into this judgment?

The snake simply said that the egg showed the way
Deep passions and desires did it bring into sway
He merely shared it with the others in the fray
They could have refused like the Devas, and stay
In Heaven, sing dance and perpetually pray.

But no, they plundered and ravaged, looted and lusted
While he, merely the egg pierced and tasted.

Chorus/Viveka:

Oh Snake! oh king! Oh Nagaraja!
You dwell in deep pits, in the earth's entrails
On your head the earth's orbit rotates on its trails
Oh! You dweller of the dark netherworld
Your hood in heaven's height unfurled

Such is the paradox of lust, desire and sexuality. The
snake has to be given its due. So friends, Adieu. The sun is
about to set. The red glow streaks across the rippling waters
of the Jamuna, touching the embracing rivers as the waves
lap and swirl in a love play, and the whirlpools suck into a
dancing vortex. The cobra slides into the tangled roots of
the Akshay Vat. Out there, on the river sand, the plywood
Neelkantha, sitting in padmasana, stands etched against the
sky. The snake curls lovingly around his sky-blue neck.

Sonjoy Dutta-Roy

Diary Poems:

BAUL STRINGS—1

How do I reach you, my soul's desire
Who my heart seeks, where my senses aspire?

The full clay vessels wait at the shores
She will carry them home, start the day's chores.

But the waltzing river, it dances and swirls
On its way with you, it winds and whirls.

And me, empty vessel, floating on its crest
As you hold me clinging, close to her breast
Moving with the ripples in a zigzagged quest.

Where do you take me, you wayward river?
Far from the shore to the ocean I quiver.

Lost in the folds of her soft embrace
The world recedes without a trace.

How do I reach you, my soul's desire
Who my heart seeks, where my senses aspire?

*In Bengal villages women use the empty clay vessels as floats for swimming and bathing in the river.
*Bauls are folk singers in rural Bengal and have their own philosophy of the body as a temple and of the divine.

BAUL STRINGS—2

Who created this palace of colours?
Here, without oil, the starlight flickers
Without electricity the moonlight glows
The sun over the horizon overflows
The breeze across the mountain blows.

For its gentle touch my heartstring quivers
For its stormy howl my *ektara** shivers
As I dance under your open sky
With the trees and the birds swaying high.

The city and its lights, its closed corridors
Its walls, its windows, and imposing doors
Have trapped me far too long.

Oh! break the lock and take me along
For your open pathways I always long.

The string musical instrument used by the Bauls of Bengal
Some of the images and symbols hark back to Lalon Fakir, the Baul singer and to Rabi Baul, Tagore as a Baul singer.

BAUL STRINGS—3

In what light will the soul's lamp be lit
So that I catch your shadows as they flit?
Oh lover, oh lunatic, oh sage, oh you
How do I catch a glimpse of you?

The thousand and one chores of the day
Had led me away and far astray
Around and round the world and its ways
Neon lights, food marts, tempting byways
On pedestals, forums, round tables and pools
In all the various universities and schools
Through rupees, dollars and the great euros
In offices, hotels and numerous bureaus
I roamed and roamed through blind alleyways.

Till your thunder and lightning broke my doorway
In a flash in the clouds your lamp was lit
And your shadows across my windows flit
And I hit the open endless freeways.

Oh in what light will the soul's lamp blaze
Oh lover, oh lunatic, oh sage, oh you
How do I catch a glimpse of you?

BAUL STRINGS—4

The time has come, oh my confined heart
For the open journey of love to start.

As the lamps within the rooms get dimmer
The stars in the skies brightly glimmer
Calling me out into the wide grasslands
Valleys, mountains, seas and islands.

Like a beggar in rags, for worldly eyes
I have left my bags for the worldly wise.

You have called me out, oh my friend
Your subtle touch, my heartstring rends.
I sing and dance to my heart's content
Oh at last the fruit has ripened
And the bud's opening has quickened
In full abandon I scatter my scent
My flavour, my flesh, to you present
The petals fly in the quickening breeze
With my honey the swarm of bees I tease

You come to me in so many forms
To test this beggar in your lover's arms
What I got from you, I return the alms.

The time has come, oh my confined heart
For the open journey of love to start.

BAUL STRINGS—5

If you think I lie caught in you net, no harm
My voice is free, my feet—vagabond
My hands in the coconut hair of your frond
Your flesh pours its milk in my cupped palm
Your sighs hold me like the waters of the pond
Quivering inside a languorous calm
Our bodies the freeways, our passion the bond
That carry us floating—in passionate embrace
To ecstatic heights of a divine solace.

From your pond to other streams, rivers and oceans
My vagabond feet find different passions.

So . . .

If you think I lie caught in your net, no harm
For what harm can there be when I lie in your arms
And you lead me to heavens through your countless charms
To celestial bliss through your myriad forms

The Comet Avatar

"The Tabloid lies on the centre table
The news will contribute to the grand fable
Of Vishnu's incarnation number ten
Oh! do not ask me what and when
But it seems somewhere close at hand
As the hourglass top is running out of sand
And the predicted symptoms of the disease
Point to the day the world will cease
The blazing sword and the snow white steed
Like a flaming Comet in tremendous speed
Shall hit the earth and wipe it clean
Ushering the new born Mahayuga in".

It was no astrologer who spoke these words
But the coffee house prophet, analyzing the discords
That stared from the page in pictures and words.
And all of us in that circular group
Could see the subtext in the journalistic scoop.

So while these headlines are still in their prime
I give you, dear friends, the prophesy in rhyme:

"Social and Spiritual life degenerate
Brahmins possess nothing to venerate
But their flimsy dirty sacred thread.

Greed lust violence will spread
Leaving everything maimed or dead.

Men and women bound in bodily pleasures
The Earth worshipped for its mineral treasures.

Mere washing will pass for purification
Villains will compete for deification.

Sacred rites wiped from the face of the earth
Truth and love shall be of no worth.

Bluff shall effectively replace learning
Robes of office give the rights for governing
Mean minded selfish individual profiteering.
Civilisation itself shall buckle and crumble
Preparing the way for the final rumble
When Vishnu as Kalki on his white steed
His flashing sword like a blazing tail
Of a comet moving in tremendous speed
Hit the earth deep in its entrails
Wiping the corrupted earth clean
Ushering the new born Mahayuga in".

But was the world ever any better
Men and women simpler and straighter?

A tale and a vision of a better time
I will narrate in metered rhyme
Follow it up rhyme by rhyme
With a twist in the tale and the vision sublime.

Tale:
"Once under a time in a better world
Two men on a strange issue quarreled
And straight they went to Yudhishthira
That apostle of learning, great Dharmavira.
On realizing that by mistake
he possessed his friend's land
This one wanted to return
every particle of sand
But the other refused to take it back
and said it straight and flat
That it did not really matter
either this way or that
So they approached the great Yudhishthira
The one and only Dharmavira
But the great man was busy with an important matter
Justice was delayed for some time later
So let us take a break, as they say on television
And watch a visual, an ethereal vision".

Vision:

This must have been around the same time
When man's best nature was still in its prime:
"A hall full of people, it was dinner time
Plates full, long ladles in hands
Feeding each other, such happy bands".

Tale continued:

"By the time our Dharmavira returned
In a strange twist our tale had turned
The two friends were still disputing the land deal
But where was the good will, concern, mutual weal?
One wanted his land back
The other refused
How was this volatile situation diffused?
Does not matter, dear friends
While the great Dharmavira delayed
Kalyuga had begun with its changed trends
And the eggs off such discords successfully laid.

Sounds familiar does it not, friends?"

Vision continued:

This must have been around the same time
When man's best nature fell from its prime:
"A hall full of people, it was dinner time

Morsels in plates, small spoons in hands
Stealing from each other, such gluttonous bands".

Kalyuga was indeed well on its way
Sounds familiar, what do you say?

"The Tabloid stares from the centre table
The news contributes to the grand fable
When Vishnu's incarnation number ten
(Oh! do not ask me what and when)
With blazing sword and the snow white steed
Like a flaming Comet in tremendous speed
Shall hit the earth and wipe it clean
Ushering the new born Mahayuga in".

The Katha Serial Saga

Well, dear listeners, I will tell you a tale
That I overheard once as I sipped a cocktail.
A great modern Guru, in professorial garb
At his eloquent best
Was narrating with zest
And let me in advance warn you, lest
You apply to it your rationality test,
A myth and a legend dipped in alcohol fumes
Arouses imagination, and reason subsumes
Willingly suspending disbelief
Opening new vistas in stark relief.

With writers, poets, academicians galore
The conversation slipped from poetry to folk lore
And as the trajectile and tangential parabole
From the oral tale to the written metaphor
Was traced from parable to the subtle symbol
One professor began in the story telling mode
How the saga of the Word as a divine fairy tale,
Hid in Prakriti's sensual code
As she with Purusha in their chamber played,
Escaped like a secret into the mortal world
Among the tribes it spread and strayed
And in earthy tongues it swirled and whirled

In numerous forms it gradually unfurled
Around man's nature and history it subtly curled
Through narration, performance and poetic diction
Through generations moved the grand fictions
Through memory, forgetting and individual additions
Of personal tales in blood inscriptions.
Into the ocean of sagas
Flow the individual ragas
Like a serial of rivers
Tributaries and brooks
Books, books and books!
In an endless chain with invisible hooks
In endless waves on the sands of time
In endless forms of reason and rhyme

Now dear listeners, I will give you the tale
As it floated to me over the cocktail:
"Once high up in the almighty heights
Shiva and Parvati had a love fight
Shiva had fooled her with a tale
Which he claimed as new, but she knew it was stale.
Pushpadanta had stolen it from their closed door
Eavesdropping as he guarded the divine corridor
And promptly whispered it to Jaya's ears
And she brought it back through Parvati's back door
Confirming Shiva's deceit, and Parvati's fears.

But when the truth was finally exposed
Pushpadanta the Gana was promptly deposed

Cursed to be born as a mortal
Deep in the Vindhya hills
The tale forgotten, and all narrative skills
Till an earth spirit, Yaksha, as Pisaca born
Jogged his memory,
And out of fragments gone and torn
The tale returned, reincarnated, reborn,
In a language close to the earth and its forms.

This Yaksha, also under a wretched curse
Would find release, his destiny reverse
If he could make the tale traverse
To Gunadhya the Gana of Parvati's second curse
(For putting for his friend a good word in
Even as Pushpadanta was paying for his sin).

Gunadhya in turn would find his release
If he could with this tale all mortals please
From eternity into time, let the tales increase.

Lest the Vidyadharas the seven tales steal
Or some get lost in memory's labyrinth
In Pisaca language did he conceal
And in his own blood the saga imprint
On the trees and leaves all over the hill.

To the king his disciples carried the tale.
Satavahana, well known for his learning and taste
Would spread the saga, knowing what was best

But it was a mission that was doomed to fail.
The king in his pride and his learning sneered
At the language, the blood, disgusted appeared.
The poor disciples silently disappeared
Back to the forest their course they steered.

Gunadhya sorrowful, ridiculed, scorned
By a competent authority so blatantly spurned
Prepared a fire that in the forest burnt
To the beasts and the birds he read from the leaves
Then into the fire he threw in the sheaves.

And the fire burnt, howled and raged
The animals tearful and transfixed gazed
Forgot to hunt, and none of them grazed.

Satavahana, the king, was with sickness attacked
Eating meat that all nutrition lacked
The hunters and physician gathered around
And finally the answer to the problem found
To the king they formally announced
That a fire burnt in the forest ground
A teller of tales read in the foreground
With the birds and beasts all around
Each leaf after reading into the fire he threw
Feeding on them the conflagration grew
The birds and beast from the pastures withdrew

Food and water did they sadly eschew
No wonder there was such undernourished meat
Served to the king at his dining seat.

Satavahana did to the forest proceed
To Gunadhya he hastened in full speed
But Gunadhya the poet had consecrated six tales
Where fire and ash and smoke prevails
The seventh remained for mortal ears
For the king to preserve for the coming years.

Let me now to you the moral expose
Of how the lone saga gathers and grows
From where it descends and how it flows
In rhythm and rhyme the future overflows
Seeking its six lost friends it goes
In fiction, poetry, performance and prose

Subtle points, dear friends, lie hidden in the frame
Of this great and wonderful tale of tales:
Born in Purusha and Prakriti's games
Spiritual values it sensually entails
But the ethereal height's intellectual abstraction
FAILS
Till it descends into mortal entrails:

Through a chain of memory and narration
Curse and release, forgetting and recollection
Revived by the quality of poetic diction

And language close to the folk imagination
And somewhere enroute, the oral tradition
Moving like an ocean, generation to generation
Seeks the signature of individual inscription
Written in blood, autobiography and fiction.

Trapped in the blood of the individual prison
The rhymed tale could find release on
Learning to correlate with nature and its denizens
Dissolving ego in ashes and flame
It would spiral its circuitous way to fame
Seeking reunion with its six lost friends
From mortal to immortal height transcends".

Post Script

And so dear listeners, enemies and friends
This is the way the saga descends
From celestial heights to mortal accents
In language, metaphor and symbol fragments
Gathers nature and its various segments
Within its folds, all the elements
And then with all its mortal load
Higher and higher it ascends.

To it I have added my own little bit
And released the saga into your ambit
For you to circulate in memory's circuit
And narrate it forward to a vaster orbit.

Sonjoy Dutta-Roy

"Contraries" for the "Prolific":

Meditations on Blake, Tagore, Yeats and Bharatrihari:

1

Renunciation can never be my path of release
And I cannot cast a cold eye on life, on death and pass
     them by
Though for receding youth there is a tear and a sigh
I still follow my heart and my flesh, wherever they please
     and tease.

But my Dear Mischievous Friend, with a thousand desires
     You plague me
And then by deprivation You subtly save me.
You make me wish that I were young again and held her in
     my arms
But neither am I young nor she desire my waning charms.
What is this game that You play with me?
You chain me to my past and yet You leave me free.
The ebb and flow of passion's waves still fret the ancient
     tossing sea
Roots still seek the labyrinthine moist in the wizened and
     gnarled tree.
Like our ancient poet I realize:

"Pursuit of pleasures only ends in pain
Still our bodies do we pamper with zest
To her body's temple we go again and again
Seeking the sanctity of her thighs and breast"
Did the spreading canopy of her hair, as she leant over my
     face
Enclose and close my senses, block the vast universe,
Or as I lost myself in them, of my self lost all trace
Was I sucked in meditation into Your elliptical embrace?
Thus, renunciation can never be my path of release
I follow You, wherever You please and tease.

2

Again as the great ancient poet said:
"What if restraint is forced on you
By circumstance, composure will ensue
Only when you at your own sweet will shunned
Temptation and attained detachment true"
Maybe that state will come, when we are our Other and our
     God
And Loves intimacies between Man and Woman
Get's reflected in the sky's thunder rumbling for the earth's
     clod
For rain to unite and make them one
Or even as the hills and ravines are embraced
By the meditative expanse of the travelling sun
As it rides the sky with its seven eternally flaming stallions
Mounting the mares of time and

Sonjoy Dutta-Roy

Begetting the foal of the world
Purusha and Prakriti in their eternal embrace whirled.

And so we swing on the tree of life, You and I
Propelled by the storm, ever higher and high,
From the tamed confines of our beds, to the wilderness of
    the sky.

3

Is it possible to achieve a self reflective complete state,
As our ancient Poet said when:
"You are your own Girl and your God as well
And through meditation create a self-engendered spell"?

Perhaps in me the Man and in me the Woman dwell
In a state of unity that is non dual
Like Humpty Dumpty, or a huge big mercury ball,
Precariously balanced on the edge of a wall
Before that shattering and fragmenting fall
And the fragments each assumed independent will
To their various routes helter skelter did they spill,
Seeking each other, the yolk and the shell.

Am I one such fragment, a minute rolling mercury ball
Little realizing my total shape, complete in itself, all in all?

4

Oh no! I know that they will not listen to you sing
They are not interested in the tunes of your string.
They only know the rant of power and money
Your song, your beard, your clothes are kind of funny
And like that mad beggar, you could be a loony.
While on the top floor, on rent, you sit with your dreams
Alone and close to your God and your thought streams
The ground level business of life goes on
The owner, his Politics, his Party, the show is on
The priests and the pundits, chanting from dusk to dawn
The lovers at their games on the sprawling lawn
You observe from your window all alone
Knowing, before long, it will all be gone
Within the vastness of the night's embrace
And in the star patterns the shapes you can trace
Of the hunter and hunted, the eternal chase
Of the twinkling diamonds' amazing maze.

Out of the window you fly
To float on the milky way
The city lights grow dimmer as high,
Higher and higher you stray
Till caught on a homeward bound plane in the sky
You circle in on the approaching runway
They angle in on you, the city lights and the highway

You brace for the impact you don't know why
Levitation over, you land with a bump and a sigh
Back through the window into your armchair's sway.

5

Back to Politics and the love games
Back to the Meetings and the Speeches
And the unending game of Names
Back to the parasites and the leeches
The quest for notoriety and fame.
Back to the Murders and Rapes
And the all exposing Video tapes.

Like the ancient Poet
I wish that I could say:
"Too long, too long in this bewildering maze
Of this world thou hast been wandering. Change thy ways"
Freed from longing and hope's enticing gaze
He tells us to learn "the quiet of the sage"
Like him again I wish I could say:
"Do not cast enticing glances at me Girl
No longer am I by these signals stirred
I did sow wild oats once, but have since changed".

No, no, I still have a long way to go
The traps and lures, my pride and ego
Still within my personality flow

Caught within the "Contraries"
I still am the "prolific"
I cannot "negate" my thousand follies
Enter the company of the holiest of holies.
Between opposing pulls tormented, Oh my friend
Teach me the balance of the symmetrical end.

Story Teller's Rhymes:

Some Parables:
With Complex Morals

When lectures turn too boring
And students turn to snoring
The balloons of Poesy we let fly
And some foxy parables we do try.

Into a web of moral contradictions
Move these complex ancient fictions.
And so you modern young men and women
Look deep into the seeds of your time
Relate the present to this past acumen
That emerges from these allegories sung in rhyme.

If there is a Law, a loop hole would be found by and by
A fine print that escapes all but the perceptive eye
And it is not only criminals who find it and try.
Often demons and villains of all forms
Are created out of the innocence of norms
As Bhasmasur's, Hiranyakasipu's, and Ravana's powers
Were generated out of Mahadeo's naive good will
In the form of the various boons that he showers
On them for their rituals, penance and mantric drills.
And so to annihilate these Frankensteins
The playful Vishnu comes with his world saving tricks

Pulls Hiranyakasipu into his powerful matrix
Of a form which is neither human, animal or divine
For it is only something "between and betwixt".
Did not Mahadeo's boon say, neither in the "day or in the
  night",
"inside or outside a dwelling", nor by "human, beast or
  divine"
Could this demon be killed, am I right?
So in a luminal fiat, did the clever playful Vishnu
Come right in time for Mankinds' and the Gods' rescue.
In the form of Narasinghavatar, half man and half beast
Grabbbed the demon at twilight, which is neither day nor
  night
On the threshold, that is neither inside or outside
On His lap, between heaven and earth, and without even a
  fight
Rips with his lion claws, Oh! What a sight!

That was gruesome, but then in a cunning and subtler way
He did once the form of Mohini assume
To entice the powerful Bhasmasur who could consume
In flames any being that strayed within his dancing palm's
  sway.
Once again it was Mahadeo's innocent naiveté
That did through a boon such a demon create.
And then when this one expressed the desire
To first on his creator, Shiva, test the fire
Poor God, He knew this was his funeral pyre.
So once again, without delay

Vishnu the playful enters the fray
He seduces the demon and leads him astray
As Mohini, the enchantress, in voluptuous form
He stirs the demon into a passionate storm
To follow each step and each nimble sway
In close and erotic imitation.
Till lost in the folds of this intimate dance
The Demon forgot in his sexual trance
That when his own palm sways over his head
Consumed into ash, he would be dead.

And so all you future demons of the coming times
Remember that for you too the clock eternally chimes
Even as power corrupts you into crimes
You will miss the fine print between the lines
The guileless God can be fooled for a while
But your rituals of power and your grand style
Is watched from the wings by other eyes
And before you know the whats from the whys
It will hit you in ways that are subtle, cunning and wise.

So, to warn you all in proper time
I weave these parables in crooked rhyme.

After the lids of the Diary Close

The Moving finger writes . . .

Where do the stories begin?
And where do they ever end?
Where do the deep roots sink in?
To what sun do the branches sway and bend?

What lies hidden in the white of a page
Ere the moving pen slants its mark?
What is left unsaid on the stage
After the curtain falls in the dark?

After the lids of the diary close
Words slip out of its hard bound hide
Stories melt out of frozen ice flows
Far into the sway of the oceanic tide.

And the story begins . . .

The seeds blend in the darkness of the wombs
Embryonic tales take ghostly shapes
Flitting in and out of myriad tombs
Wrapped in the white of papyrus drapes.

Love and war lie embalmed in the seeds
In the stark route of the Mahaprasthana
  by the wayside drop all ambitions and needs.
And the great Vyasa whose loins fathered forth
Tales and yarns in endless breeds
Flowing in my blood and in your deeds.
Meditates in the quiet of silent battle fields
On how central were those acts of love
Where a savage hermit living in the wild
Was called into the royal alcove
To perform in the darkness
  with two maidens, civilized and mild
A primal act
  to embed deep into a virgin grove
Seeds of a future, progeny and child.

Did the great Vyasa, the hermit sage, austere, wild and wise
In his deepest thoughts realize
How each thrust and parry
Held in tense and intense balance
Forces of Eternity in a complex History
Of a nation springing from His loin's story
Holding
Ecstacy and Agony in a trance
The savage and the civilized, passion and reason
  in an uneasy séance.

He Remembers . . .

The shock in Ambika beautiful eyes
As she saw the bearded and matted hair,
    the fearful, and naked guise
Of the sage whose loin cloth,
     started to swell and rise
At the sight of such a polished prize.
In horror she closed her lovely eyes
Being innocent and not at all worldly wise

Chorus:

By blindness and passion was innocence deflowered
By such forces would future events be powered
And a blind king was with the sceptre empowered.

He Remembers . . .

The colour of Ambalika's lovely face
Change in horror to a deathly pale
At the thought of an uncouth savage embrace
Of an aroused and lusty primal male
Ere he pulsed into her virgin cove
Her sophisticated and private treasure trove
The seeds of a royal princely race.

Chorus:

In fear, lust and disgust was innocence deflowered
By such forces would future events be powered
And a pale king was with the sceptre empowered.

But where did it go wrong?

He remembers the third story:

Ambalika, on the second fateful night, cunning and clever,
Knowing that in the secret dark
Maybe it is all the same, the curves, crevices and the quiver,
Puts a royal maid in her place, with an innate sexual spark
Who has none of the royal snobbery
Or fine delicate upper caste ways
That refine sexuality's hard core truths
    dwelling in the netherworld's secret alleyways
She was a match for our wild sadhu
Earthy and sensual, she was a natural, without a taboo
No blue blood in her veins,
    she was a daughter of the forest
And embraced our Vyasa, without fuss or ado,
And held him tight, gave full permit.
It was a night of pure pleasure, without any rest
For was not Vyasa's origin rooted in the conquest
Of a fisherwoman's body by a wandering hermit.

Chorus and Final Moral of the Story:

But the child born of this union, dear Vidura
Forever deprived, forever ignored
    while the blind and the pale ruled

Was Vyasa's statement of natural justice
The voice of the people, though overruled
Remaining as a subtext, and well underscored
Potent and strong, always and forever,
    against the rule of injustice.

Notes on the Poems

1.) In ***The Snake Story*** I have used a Folk Purana from Madesvara, It is a women's retelling of the genesis myth. I have added contemporary twists and a personal angle in the tone.

2.) In ***The Comet Avatar*** I have used the myth of the tenth incarnation of Vishnu in the form of a comet with a flaming tail destroying the present yuga (age) and ushering in the next yuga which is the Mahayuga. The predictions of course have been given a little twist by me for readers and listeners to discover familiar truths about the times we are living in. I have also used the story of the two friends approaching Yudhishthira from the **Mahabharata**. It is a little noticed interpolating story tucked into the grand epic. The story of the ideal feast and its transformation has been used in Buddhist texts to illustrate the changed values in contemporary times and highlighting the earlier selfless values in an age of innocence.

3.) ***The Katha Serial Saga*** uses the frame story from Kathasaritasagar (originally the Brihatkatha), where stories created by Shiva for Parvati as part of their love play and entertainment are stolen by eavesdroppers and slowly make their way through various layers down into the world of the folk and into the natural world. Interestingly, in the remembering and retelling of the stories they assume new dimensions and also regain access back into the divine fold from where they descended. The curse of forgetting one's original stories is also lifted (the eavesdroppers were cursed by Parvati) and the storytelling chain continues retaining cultural continuity into contemporary times. To me this story is specially significant in the Post Colonial context where Western education has been seen as a curse that has broken the continuity in our chain of narratives.

4.) **Some Parables: With Complex Morals** uses the stories of the creation of two demons Bhasmasur and Hiranyaksipu, by boons granted to them by Lord Shiva (Mahadeo) as gift for their single minded meditative and ritualistic devotion to him and which they start misusing against the Gods and humanity. This calls for Vishnu's entering the fray and ultimately destroying them using sometimes crude and sometimes subtle means.

5.) **After the Lids of The Diary Close** uses one of the origin tales of the Mahabharata. Satyavati, a fisherwoman conceived the sage Vyasa through an illegitimate union with a wandering hermit Parashar. Later king Shantanu took a fancy for her and married her. Their son Vichitravirya married to Ambika and Ambalika dies childless. Shantanu too had a son Bhisma through a premarriage union with Ganga. To continue the royal lineage Bhisma was called forth after the death of Vichitravirya, but Bhisma had taken a vow of chastity.

Thus Vyasa's services were called forth. Vyasa, the mythical poet of the Mahabharata, was a wild hermit uncivilized in appearance. The royal princesses had serious problems with him. The rest of the story has been fleshed out by me in the poem.

About The Author

Sonjoy Dutta-Roy teaches in the Department of English Studies, University of Allahabad, India. His Ph.D dissertation was on the poetry of W.B Yeats and T.S Eliot. He published his first paper in the *Yeats Eliot Review* that is published from Arkansas, U.S.A followed by one in the *Indian Journal of English Studies* (edited at that time by K.Ayappa Panniker). This was followed by another paper in the *Journal of Modern Literature* published from Temple University, Philadelphia and another from *Yeats Eliot Review* Arkansas. In 1995-96 he was a Senior *Fulbright Visiting Fellow* at the Louisiana State University, Baton Rouge U.SA working with Professor James Olney (editor The Southern Review) on the relationship between Poetry and Autobiography. This resulted in the publication of his book *(Re) Constructing the Poetic Self: Tagore, Whitman Yeats, Eliot,* (Pencraft International). *This*

book was selected by the Human Resource and Development Ministry for distribution in University and other libraries in India. He has been researching on the Poetic, Performative and Fictive Narratives in India, and has lectured on the subject at UC Berkeley, SUNY Stonybrook, Nassau Community College, The Indian Institute of Advanced Study, Shimla (where he was a Research Associate) Jadavapur University and Allahabad University. Excerpts from his work have been published in *Studies in Humanities and Social Sciences* and *Summerhill*, which are major journals appearing from the Institution. He has been a Fulbright Visiting Professor at University of California, Berkeley in 2004-2005 where he taught a Graduate course on narratives in India. This research on narratives has subtle connections with his book of poems, from which he has read at all these places and also at the Indo Irish Poetry reading at the Sahitya Academy, New Delhi. Sonjoy Dutta-Roy is a poet. Two of his poetic collections, *The Absent Words,* (1998) and *Into Grander Space* (2005) were published by Writers Workshop, Kolkata and received good reviews in major newspapers and Poetry journals in India.

Sonjoy Dutta-Roy has been actively involved in theatre. He has acted in plays and recently directed 6 plays under the joint sponsorship of the University of Allahabad and the North Central Zone Cultural Centre. His Group, the Theatre for Peace group performed Karnad's "Hayavadana", Mohan Rakesh's "One Day in Ashadh", Mahesh Elkunchwar's, "Autobiography" and "Eighteen Days", (based on the Mahabharata, self composed narrative), Mahesh Dattani's "Tara" and Rabindranath Tagore's "Dak Ghar" (The Post Office) in 2008-2011. These plays have now become an annual feature to which the Allahabad theatre going public looks forward to.